ALL BARCELONA

Text, photographs, lay-out and reproduction, entirely designed and created by the Technical Department of EDITORIAL ESCUDO DE ORO, S.A.

Rights of total or partial reproduction and translation reserved.

Copyright of this edition for photographs and text:
© EDITORIAL ESCUDO DE ORO, S.A.

2nd Edition, March 1980

I.S.B.N. 84-378-0021-8

Spanish (Paperback)	84-378-0623-2	Spanish (Cased)	84-378-0624-0
French (Paperback)	84-378-0625-9	French (Cased)	84-378-0626-7
English (Paperback)	84-378-0627-5	English (Cased)	84-378-0628-3

Dep. Legal B. 951-XXIII

editorial **escudo de oro, s.a.** Palaudarias, 26 - Barcelona, 4 - Spain
Impreso en España - Printed in Spain
F.I.S.A. Palaudarias, 26 - Barcelona-4

"Harbour of courtesy, shelter of foreigners, hospital of the poor, home of the brave, revenge of the oppressed and place of faithful friendship, unique in setting and beauty". This was the definition of Barcelona Cervantes lent to his noble Knight. As you will see, Cervantes was right in his judgement.

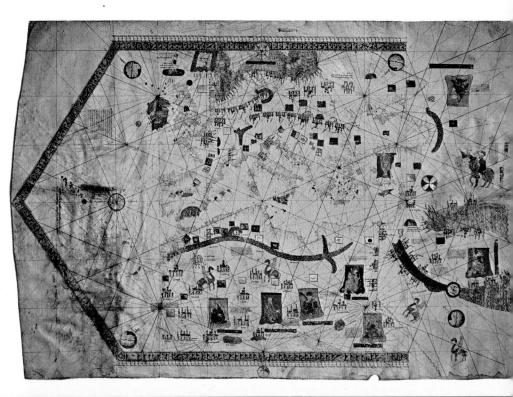

Map of the Mediterranean by Gabriel de Valseca. It dates back to 1439 and is the oldest sea map existing in Spain. It belonged to Amerigo Vespucci. To be seen in the Maritime Museum.

THE IBERIAN LAYE

Present-day Barcelona, the city resting on the maternal lap of mount Tibidabo and Montjuich and extending as far as the sea, affectionately fondled by the arms of the rivers Besós and Llobregat, according to some historical sources is supposed to have been the Iberian city of Laye some two thousand years ago. Tradition has it that of the primitive townshipa of the tribes of Laye the Carthaginian general Hamilcar Barca laid the first stone of Barcelona as it is known today. This first stone was to be followed by many others for the very city of Rome susequentely granted Barcelona its recognition and citizenship. On his part, Athaulf made the city the capital of the Visigothic monarchy.

But Barcelona, already won over to Christendom, was subsequentely occupied by the Arabs and later by the Franks. This gave rise to the Hispanic March which was immediately fractioned into a large number of counties destroying the unity which William the Villous took upon himself to restore. And after unification, independence came, and with it the promotion to the status of capital of the kingdom of Catalonia-Aragón. This was an era of expansion and splendour.

It was under the reigns of Jaime II and Peter III that Barcelona acquired her outstanding personality which Cervantes had in mind when he dedicated to the city the words which open this book.

THE RAMBLAS

The Ramblas, the city's most popular avenue, extends from Puerta de la Paz —at the foot of the Columbus memorial— to Catalonia Square. This is actually a rather short stretch for a city which has acquired giant proportions, but it is a stretch along which the true flavour of genuine Barcelona is still preserved. To stroll along the Ramblas, to plunge into its stream, is to enter Pandora's box which releases ageold memories; it is the direct experience of the sensitive and educated Barcelona of today and yesterday, of yesterday and tomorrow. For Barcelona, active and untiring, carefully cultivates the synopsis of its book and newspaper stands, practically open around the clock, as a kind of tacit system of supply of food for thought. And next to these newspaper stands there are the modern flower stands. They offer the flowers popularly associated with the name of this section of the Ramblas. And amid books and flowers, at the feet and in the branches of the plane-trees, birds. Birds fluttering freely in the branches of the trees, and less fortunate, but more colourful and valuable birds on display in cages at the very feet of these trees.

But you, guest of Barcelona, would be wrong in assuming that Barcelona is just —as if it were little— flowers, birds and books. It is true that you will find these three elements in the most unexpected corners of the city. But still, you would be wrong because Barcelona not only pays tribute to nature through its birds and flowers and to culture though its books, but it also pays tribute —and with great enthusiasm— to the customs of its

The Ramblas is the main avenue of old Barcelona. Their endearingly traditional pattern of trees, birds, papers and flowers enter into a fundamental and automatic symbiosis with the uninterrupted flow of passers-by at any time of day or night. Strolling along the Ramblas is breathing the most typical flavour of the city of yesterday and today.

The Patio of the ancient hospital of Santa Cruz and San Pablo conserves all its air of a medieval world inside the hub of a great city like an oasis for the visitor.

The Sardana «Dance of a people that loves and progresses holding hands».

forefathers. Barcelona —nobody can deny it— is a city which boldly accepts the challenges of the future without losing sight of its traditions. Thus, if we leave the Ramblas and turn to the right towards any of the many little squares of the Gothic area, if we are lucky to go there on a public holiday, we may see people dancing in a circle, holding one another's hands. They are dancing the Sardana, the dance which the Catalan poet Juan Maragall defined as:

The Sardana is the most beautiful
of all the group dances.
It is the dance of a people marching
forward holding one another's hands.

The green geometry of Plaza Real
surrounds one of the most typical
squares of Barcelona. Centrally
located and yet intimate, there
is a distinct 19th century touch
about its regular colonnades,
its palmtrees and its fountain
in the middle. Note the street lamps
designed by Gaudí. On Sunday
morning Plaza Real is the
meeting place of stamp collectors.

PALACE OF THE PROVINCIAL COUNCIL

This building has two entrances, the one built by Pere Blay in the 17th century leading through the actual valuable Gothic facade of the building in Calle del Obispo Irurita Street. This part is from the 15th century and is decorated with gargoyles, latticework and a splendid medallion of Saint George, all of which is the work of Pere Johan.

Inside the Building, particularly remarkable features are the chapel —with its splendid front piece of Saint George, patron of Catalonia, the orange tree patio dating back to the 16th century and one of the most beautiful and peaceful parts of the building, the gilt hall with the portraits of the Catalan Kings by Ariosto, and Saint George's Hall.

THE TOWN HALL

Here we are already in the middle of the Gothic area, surrounded by a wealth of medieval monuments. We are contemplating the town hall with its Gothic structure unfortunately disfigured by a neoclassical facade. The actual facade of the town hall in still visible on one side, in Calle de la Ciudad. It is the work of Arnau Bargués and represents a remarkable specimen of secular Catalan Gothic.

After entering the building through the main door, a broad staircase

Provincial Council Palace.
Staircase and gallery.

Provincial Council Palace.
Orange tree Patio.

leads to the Gothic gallery. Opposite this structure we find the chronicles hall decorated by José María Sert. This hall communicates with the Buen Consejo Chapel near which we find the so-called Salón de Ciento, built in 1373 by Master Pere Llobet. A lateral door leads to the less valuable hall of the Regent Queen dating back to the 19th century. Needless to say, the town hall, as all the other buildings in the Gothic district, features many other valuable extensions which it would be too long to enumerate here. The interested visitor will enjoy discovering them by himself and in the process he will discover to his considerable satisfaction many unique details of decoration, for in the Gothic district each house or street corner holds in store a surprise for those who are curious enough to look for details other than those superficially pointed out by a tourist guide.

On one side of the Town Hall, at the end of Calle Hércules we find the Church of the Saints Justo and Pastor, a Gothic work including Saint Felix Chapel which retains the privilege of the so-called Sacramental Testament.

This privilege is still available to the inhabitants of Barcelona. If a citizen has made a verbal will in the presence of two witnesses, these merely have to swear this will in front of the altar of this chapel for their statement to acquire the status of a notarial document.

The severe lines of the Salón de Ciento, closely associated with the history of Catalonia. It was built in 1373 by Master Pere Llobet.

Obispo Irurita Street, in the heart of the Gothic area, offers its petrified scenery which still looks as it must have looked in the Middle Ages.

PLAZA DEL REY

Only a few steps from the Provincial Council Palace we find Plaza del Rey, a square surrounded by high walls. Its grandeur and beauty are such that visitors have been found to lower their voices to a respectful whisper when entering the square. One cannot help feeling that Plaza del Rey is one of the few genuine monuments of history.

The corner between Plaza del Rey and Bajada de la Cárcel, in the foreground of this monument of history, is formed by the Clariana-Padellás house, transferred stone by stone to its present location after it had to be pulled down when the present Vía Layetana avenue was built. This house which combines Gothic tradition with the taste of the Renaissance today houses the Museum of City History. Its subsoil contains valuable remains of the Roman-Christian Barcelona, of the 4th century.

But the most valuable building of Plaza del Rey is the Royal Palace, also known as Palace of the Counts of Barcelona because it was first the place of residence of the Catalan Counts and subsequently became the Palace of the Kings of Aragon. Originally, the Palace was built in Romanesque style in the 11th century. Only in the 14th century, the Royal Chapel of Santa Agueda, a Gothic chapel with a slender octogonal tower was added. It occupies the whole of the right hand side wing. The chapel houses the altar-piece done by Jaime Huguet —the most famous catalan painter of the 15th century— for Constable Don Pedro of Portugal, pretender to the crown of Aragon.

Plaza del Rey by night.
This is a genuine gem of world
Gothic and the theatre of one of the most
glorious pages in the history
of the discovery of the New World.

The façade of the Town Hall.

Town Hall. Chronicles hall.
Its decoration may be
regarded as the greatest
work of José María Sert.

Inside the Royal Palace, to the left, we find the spectacular Tinell hall. This is a vast rectangular hall —17 metres wide and 35 metres long— the present structure of which dates back to the 2nd half of the 14th century. This splendid hall consists of six huge semicircular arches sustaining the beams of the roof. Its walls built prior to the 14th century have small Romanesque window openings of rather primitive appearance. These openings are small indeed, but saturated with a long and fascinating history. These Romanesque openings still filled with Mediterranean light witnessed nearly five centuries ago the unique

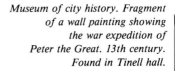

Museum of city history. Fragment
of a wall painting showing
the war expedition of
Peter the Great. 13th century.
Found in Tinell hall.

Museum of city history.
Altar-piece of the Constable, 1465.
Saint George. By Jaime Huguet.

Museum of city history.
Miniature painting from
the comment on the «Usatges».
Jaime Marquillas (15th century).

Museum of city history. Bronze statue
from the Ist century,
known as «Venus of Barcelona».

Museum of city history.
Roman marble head of
Empress Agrippina. Ist century.

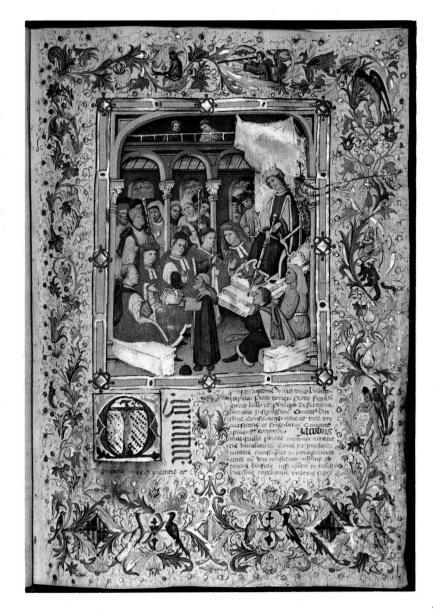

event of Columbus' return from his voyage to the New World. There he delivered the proofs of his adventures to the Catholic Kings who had travelled to Barcelona impatient to satisfy themselves as to the facts of this unprecedented achievement.

On one side of the same Square, we have the Archives of The Crown of Aragon, also known as the former Palace of the Lieutenant which dates back to the 16th century. Apart from sheltering an invaluable wealth of historical records, the visitor will admire the splendid panelled ceiling of its main staircase. Dreamers will remember that for some time this building was the residence of the most famous of the Dukes of Gandía, Saint Francis Borgia.

Now, to get a short spell of rest after so many testimonies of history and ancient architecture, we recommend a visit to the nearby intimate building of Marés Museum with its valuable and varied collection of sculptures covering all the styles from the round and bombastic shapes of Hellenic female nudes to the austere and vigorous sculptures of Spanish artists.

Inside view of the Royal Chapel of Saint Agueda. In the background, the famous altar-piece of the Constable.

The altar-piece of the Constable. Thus named because Constable Don Pedro of Portugal had it painted by Jaime Huguet in the 15th century.

A broad view of Tinell hall. It consists of six huge semi-circular arches and dates back to the 2nd half of the 14th century.

Ramón Berenguer Square. Impressive night view of the equestrian statue of the Count and King of Catalonia silhouetted against the background of Saint Agueda Chapel in a smooth merging of the monument into its surroundings.

The Cathedral majestically stands dominating the whole of the Gothic quarter.

THE CATHEDRAL

Only a stone's throw from the Archives of the Crown of Aragon, we find one of the proudest Gothic cathedrals of Spain and possibly of the world.

As we are again in Obispo Irurita Street, let us enter the Cathedral through the Romanesque door of the chapel of Santa Lucía. This chapel —which shelters the sepulchre of Bishop Arnau de Gurp who had it built in the 13th century —is but a first impression of the many valuable works of art which are waiting for our visit.

We now proceed to the cloister of the Cathedral, in the purest Gothic style, with its corporation chapels and its garden in the middle, a true refuge of peace. In the chapter hall a small cathedral museum has been arranged so that none of the many gems of art are overlooked by the visitors. Despite its modest scale, this museum is most valuable as it features many paintings and codices as well as medieval sculptures. Among the exhibits attention should be drawn to, The Stone by Bartolomé Bermejo, a masterpiece from the end of the 15th century.

There are two further Gothic doors in the cloister, one of them leading into the church. After having penetrated into the church through this door, we start our visit from the right. In the first place we find the chapel of the Sacrament with the sepulchre of Saint Olegario, featuring a splendid lying statue of the Saint, and above all the famous Christ of Lepanto. This sculpture from the 15th century was carried by John of Hapsburg on his flagship in the naval battle which resulted in the supremacy of Christendom over the Turkish empire. The body of the Christ of Lepanto is slightly inclined to one side the legend being that he had to avoid the projectile of one of the enemy's guns.

After contemplating in the following lateral chapels the altar painting of Saints Cosme and Damián and the sarcophagus of Saint Raimundo de Peñafort, we are at the foot of the main altar, a work of the 14th. century made of gilt wood which rests on the crypt of Saint Eulalia. After going down a few steps, we are in front of the patron Saint of Barcelona, a white marble sepulchre with an impressive sculpture from the beginning of the 14th century, no less

The sober lines of the Puerta de la Piedad.

In the evening the Cathedral has a magical look.

splendid than the choir of the cathedral, situated in the center of the main nave. This choir bears the tangible testimonies of history, for on the back rest of each choir chair we can read the name and see the coat of arms of the Kings who sat there in 1519 when emperor Charles 5th. presided over the first chapter of the order of the Golden Fleece, a gathering of the most distingui-shed and noble characters of European chivalry.

After admiring the pulpit and countless other minor details which catch our eyes, let us visit the sacristy to see the crown of King Martín the Humane and, apart from other age old historical objects, the famous Gothic monstrance with the golden fleece of Charles 5th. as the main ornament.

And before leaving the cathedral through Saint Ivo's Door, the oldest part of the church, let us cast a last glance on this prayer made in stone, on this miracle of faith, and we see, aware of the age-old history of the building, how the multi-coloured light rests softly on the hard marble, how it lights the shining gold and gives a noble appearance to the eroded stones.

The archdeacon's house. Partival view of the ground floor with a fountain in the middle.

THE ARCHDEACON'S HOUSE

This building of outstanding beauty was erected in the 16th century by the archdeacon Luis Desplá who had it built on ancient Roman foundations. In the last century the archdeacon's house was extended to include the deacon's house, also from the 16th century, which today houses the historical archives of the city. Indeed, an adequate framework for a museum containing the invaluable written records of a peerless city.

The march of History has stopped, respecting a magical world, in the Square of Ramón Berenguer.

*Museum of city history. Wall painting
from the Paleochristian basilica
of Barcelona. 6th century.*

*Museum of city history. Diana.
A fine but unfortunately
truncated sculpture.*

PLAZA NUEVA

Before completing the visit to
the so-called Gothic district, and as
a rest from so many Gothic monuments projecting into the Christian
sky as prayers made stone, without
leaving the district, we may contemplate in Plaza Nueva, near the cathedral, one of the fragments of the
wall which surrounded the ancient
Barcino. This is a piece of wall attributed to the first century but which
seems to have been restored at some
later date after the attacks of the
Barbarian hordes.

*Museum of city history. Roman marble
bust which is supposed
to represent the effigy of Antoninus
Pius. 2nd century.*

CATALONIA SQUARE

Any city worthy of this name has a square which is a kind of centre point generating all the vital bloodstream of the city, a kind of powerful heart. The centre point is also a place of contemplation of achievements, waiting for further challenges to be met.

Barcelona's centre point is Catalonia Square. A vast circus worthy of a great city, with fountains and a flower clock, with lawns, sculptures by Clará, with noise but also with pigeons and children. Catalonia Square is the border between the old and the new part of the city. On Catalonia Square Barcelona changes its face and acquires new features which the reader will get to know at a later stage, for his visit to the old part of the city is not yet completed. First of all, he has to return to the Columbus memorial, this time not with his back turned to the memorial facing the Ramblas. He should now stand on the left side of the memorial, looking to the sea. Thus, he will discover a further and equally fascinating aspect of the city.

Night view of Catalonia Square, so far the central point of the general lay-out of the city.

Catalonia Square with the Paseo de Gracia on the right.

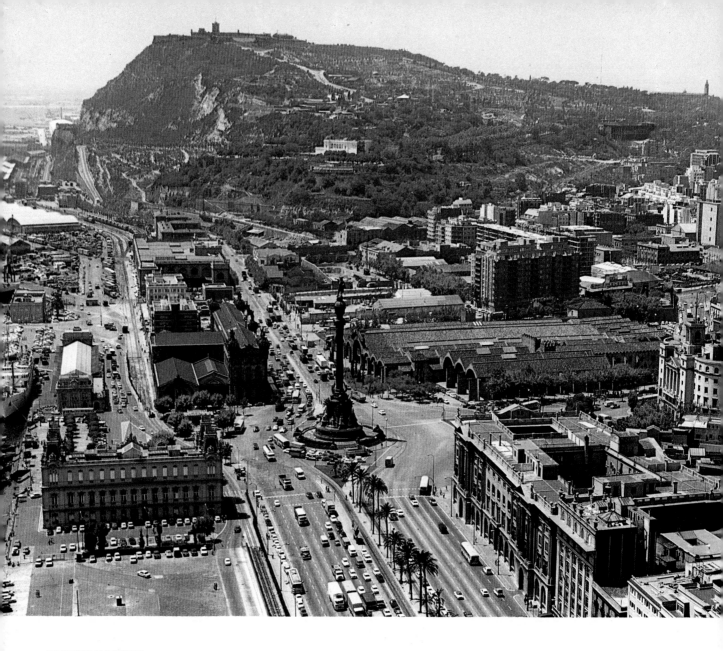

MERCED BASILICA

The present basilica situated on the left of Columbus Promenade is a late version of the initial Gothic church which formed a single building with the original house of the Merced order. This order was founded by Saint Pedro Nolasco after a vision of the virgin and was devoted to the task of obtaining the release of prisoners.

The facade of the present church is in the late Baroque style and has a Renaissance door on one side. One object of particular value is the sculpture of the virgin over the main altar. This polychromic wooden sculpture from the 14th century is attributed to the sculptor Pedro Moragas.

The port area, busy, alive and colourful, it stretches at the feet of the mountain of Montjuïc.

Our Lady of La Merced, patron saint of Barcelona. Polychromed sculpture from the 14th century.

STOCK EXCHANGE PALACE

On one side of Paseo de Isabel II, the extension of Columbus Promenade, we find the stock exchange palace, a neoclassical building erected towards the end of the 18th century by the architect Juan Soler Faneca. It houses the exchange hall with its three Gothic naves.

Stock exchange. Main staircase.

*Stock Exchange. Exchange hall with its
three famous Gothic naves
dating from the 14th century.*

MARINE AND CULINARY BARCELONA

To the right of Columbus Promenade we have the port of Barcelona which under Jaime I controlled the Mediterranean. And next to this part of Barcelona, we have one of the areas most representative of Barcelona's cuisine. For Barcelona, as a Mediterranean city is a sensual city. Its sensuality covers the whole range from intellectual love of music to the material love of gastronomy. Therefore, it is not surprising that one of the most popular dishes in Barcelona is "Zarzuela", known in its more substantial version as "Opera", two dishes comprising fish and seafood and differentiated by the presence or absence of half a lobster. This half lobster is what raises the works of Chapí and Vives to the level of scores by Verdi and Wagner and since Barcelona has managed to unite music and gastronomy, who would be surprised to learn that Barcelona has also been the first place to introduce cuisine as a means of communication? For it was in Barcelona where the first Spanish treatise on cuisine was printed, the well-known book by Roberto de Nola, published in 1477

Partial view of the eminently commercial Port of Barcelona.

The Beach of the Barceloneta. At the end of the sea walk.

Some of the rich ingredients of fish cuisine.

In spite of all this, Barcelona does not have any dishes entirely of its own. Its cuisine is one of adaptation and is based, as Catalonian cuisine as a whole, on two ingredients inherited from ancient Rome: oil and garlic. Needless to say, these primary ingredients have been subsequently supplemented with the contributions of the Arabs and later with the spices from America. Barcelona's cuisine is both rich and varied, but since we are already in the Barceloneta area, our advice is that the visitor should taste some fish specialities, preferably seasoned with "allioli" or "romesco". He may also ask for "suquet de peix" and thus feel like a seaman for this is the typical dish of local fishermen. And while we are giving advice, we might as well recommend "popets" (octopus) and "musclos" (mussels), not to forget the "zarzuela" as mentioned before and its special version known as "ópera".

Meat and sausages also provide many rich combinations, thus "escudella i carn d'olla", a kind of hotpot including ingredients ranging from the humble and simple potato to the sophisticated and rich "pilota"; "botifarra amb rovellons", i.e. sausage with mushrooms; "seques (beans) amb botifarra"; rabbit with "allioli", "bacalla a la llauna" (salt cod) and so forth, down to a speciality apparently as simple as bread with tomato and ham which in Barcelona is a true monument of rich simplicity.

More typical are local pastry products such as "cremes cremades", "tortells", "mató" and many other pastry items which are particularly appreciated by the local population, to such an extent that it may be said that there is one typical pastry product for practically all the major festivals.

However, Barcelona is something more than possible dishes. Those succulent dishes capable of satisfying the most varied and exacting palates. Barcelona is a city of Restaurants. A city in which each dish has its home, some very distinct places which have been selected by the exacting local gourmets of the city.

Those gourmets who possess a special sense of direction for discovering the place, often more typical than elegant, in which a typical ''cap i pota'' (cold meats in sauce) or a simple ''bacallá (bacalao) a la llauna'' (salt cod) are served, will experience a culinary work of art. An art that a Catalan compares to a good performance in the Liceo.

Butifarra, sausages with beans, «habas a la catalana» and «paella a la marinera». Three dishes that have broken gastronomic frontiers and which are worthy representatives of the Catalan cuisine.

View of the Basilica of Santa María del Mar, one of the proudest achievements of Catalan Gothic. Particular features are the splendid porch and the two lofty towers framing the façade.

BASILICA SAINT MARY DEL MAR

The basilica Saint Mary del Mar is the spiritual centre of a district with a long fishermen's tradition. This large Gothic church built in the 14th century is regarded as the greatest specimen of medieval Catalan architecture characterized by the extreme simplification of line.

This church has been described by Pierre Lavedan as "the most beautiful victory of mind over matter which has been achieved in the Middle Ages". And indeed only mind is powerful enough to sustain the enormous vault — with only few columns separated from one another by the unique distance of 13 metres —; and only the strongest inspiration can have designed such an accurate arrangement of the windows that the light falling through the stained glass panels, of which that of the Last Judgement and of the coronation of the virgin are the most valuable, follows an accurately arranged pattern.

Inside the Basilica of Santa María del Mar. The sober ornamentation and the serious simplicity of the columns make up a really marvellous architectural scene.

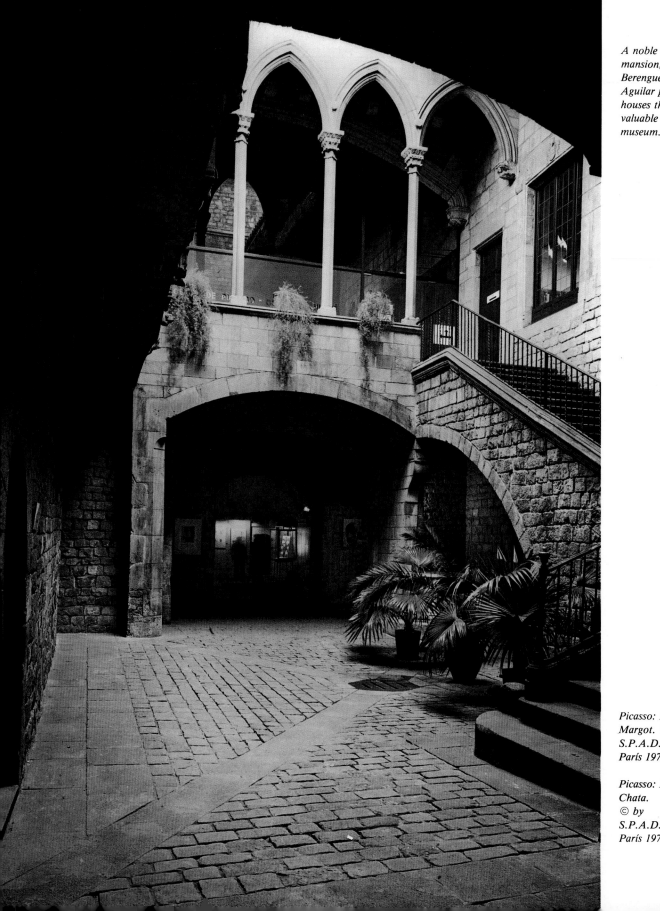

A noble
mansion, the
Berenguer de
Aguilar palace,
houses the
valuable Picasso
museum.

Picasso: La
Margot. © by
S.P.A.D.E.M.
París 1970.

Picasso: La
Chata.
© by
S.P.A.D.E.M.
París 1970.

MONCADA STREET AND ITS PICASSO MUSEUM

Next to the district known as Borne we find Calle Moncada, regarded as the most distinguished street of the city for almost six centuries, from the 13th to the 18th century. It is flanked by the palaces of famous and influential Catalan families of the past. At number 20 we find the Dalmases Palace, built in the middle of the 17th century, with its remarkable Baroque main staircase; number 25 is Cervelló house with a Gothic façade. This is followed by the houses of the Baron of Castellet, of the Counts of Santa Coloma with its famous Patio with a Gothic gallery from the 15th century; by the house of the Marquis of Llió with its museum of ecclesiastical robes and finally to mention only the most remarkable specimens, the palace of Berenguer de Aguilar which today houses the Picasso Museum the visit of which is a must for any lover of art for it features the world's largest collection of works by the painter who was born in Málaga but who acquired his artistic education in Barcelona. His love for Barcelona is so deep that he gave the city 900 of his works, coveted by many countries, which cover the whole of his artistic career.

Picasso: The Harlequin.

*Picasso: his dove, world-famous
version of the human yearning
for peace.
© by S.P.A.D.E.M. Paris 1970.*

*Picasso: One of his numerous
versions and interpretations
of Las Meninas by Velázquez.
© by Cercle d'Art. Paris 1970.*

CIUDADELA PARK

Only a few metres from Moncada Street we find what under Philip V (first half of the 18th century) was a bulwark, subsequently pulled down to provide space for the grounds and facilities designed to house the pavillions of the world exhibition of 1888. Hence the 19th century impression which the visitor gains from this park although subsequent alterations have changed its original appearance to a large extent. Of the initial buildings, only two palaces and the church have survived. They are situated around a placid pond dominated by Llimona's statue "Desolation", surrounded by water lilies.

The largest building in the park is the former arsenal, today housing the modern art museum which shows the works of the greatest painters and sculptors after the 18th century. There are paintings by Fortuny, Rusiñol, Nonell, Zuloaga and Solana, and sculptures by Llimona, Clará, Gargallo, Hugué and Rebull. The museum also includes a gallery with sketches of Vich cathedral by José María Sert and a valuable coin collection.

Cascade in the Ciudadela park. This construction provides a harmonious combination of neoclassical lines with the playful decorative effect of water.

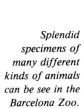
Splendid specimens of many different kinds of animals can be see in the Barcelona Zoo.

The other building, a bare brick construction, is the work of Domenech i Montaner and houses the municipal museum of natural history with a collection of stuffed animals and the Martorell museum specializing in petrography, mineralogy and paleontology.

The zoological gardens of Barcelona, situated in Ciudadela park, is one of the world's most advanced zoos. Recently built, it has incorporated the best features of existing zoos. Although modest in size, it is rich in unique exhibits which make a visit an unforgettable experience. The visitor can admire a broad range of animals living in apparent liberty, with specimens as rare as ''Snowflake'' the white Gorilla, in addition to other fascinating animals such as the performing dolphins.

We would recommend any visitor of Barcelona not only to visit the

*Modern Art Museum. Ramón Casas:
«Scene in Paris».*

*The Modern
Art Museum.
F. Masriera:
«Invierno de
1882».*

The lady with the umbrella, a remembrance of 19th century Barcelona.

The work by Llimona «Desolación» is found situated in front of the Modern Art Museum.

All styles of sculpture have a place in this enclosure, another sample of the varied artistical production that is housed in the Park.

Modern Art Museum. Fortuny: «The Vicar's office» (fragment). ▷

zoo, but also to explore Ciudadela park. Also recommended are the other parks of Barcelona. In this way the visitor will discover the countless details which cannot be listed individually. On a leisurely walk of exploration, the visitor will not only discover but understand and feel the memories suggested by monuments such as the "Lady with the umbrella", a genuine symbol of the city.

And with the nostalgia of this encounter with himself, the visitor will leave Ciudadela park, passing by the "Triumphal Arch".

The triumphal Arch presides over a beautiful urban perspective.

THE PALACE OF CATALAN MUSIC

The Palace of Catalan Music, near Vía Layetana, is one of the strangest buildings which you are ever likely to see. Surprising as it may be on account of the apparently uncontrolled fancy of its architect — Domenech i Montaner — it nevertheless gives a faithful impression of Barcelona's modern style era in the last century. Visitors to Barcelona should go to the Palace of Music — headquarters of the famous "Orfeó Catalá" — to listen to a concert and to witness the surprising harmony of two factors apparently as heterogeneous as the sound of the concert and the appearance of the building.

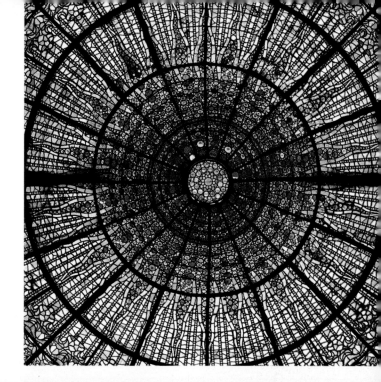

The Palace of Catalan Music. Skylight of the concert hall.

Palace of Catalan Music. Hall and main staircase.

THE BULLFIGHT

On his way the Sacred Family Church where he will meet with a new world of unexpected proportions, the visitor should take a look at the picturesque and unique world of the bullfight. If he enters the so called monumental bullring which is situated on his way to the Sacred Family Church and is the bigger of the two bullrings of Barcelona, as suggested by its name, he will become acquainted with the physical reality of the ring, the barrier, the tiers, the "banderillas", the clapping hands and the "olé" shouts; but above all he will be in a position to imagine the feeling of a man faced with possible death, and he will understand that life sometimes seems to come to a standstill in the moments between life and death, while the sun brightens its light in the blood-soaked ring; soaked with blood which — in the fraction of a second between an "olé" and a cry of terror — may become the lifeblood of the bullfighter.

The ritual of the bullfight begins with the parade of the bullfighters and their assistants to the sound of bugles.

THE BARCELONA OF GAUDI

Barcelona is a city of cities. And among these cities making up Barcelona as a whole, one of the most typical parts, almost comparable to the Gothic district, is the Barcelona of Gaudí. A Barcelona the capital of which is Sacred Family Church. An unfinished church the crypt of which shelters the remains of the great architect.

In front of the Sacred Family Church whoever is contemplating the building — of which only one of the planned three facades, that of Nativity, is completed — is reduced to silence. It is a complex of stone, iron, glass and clay, considered a masterpiece by some and regarded as a nightmare by others. Many opinions have been voiced about Gaudí: some have praised him as a unique artist whereas others cringe at the mere sound of his name. There have been indeed many different opinions, but never did any visitor of the monument disclaim an opinion.

But Gaudí not only astounds us with his greatest work; the architect from Reus had the gift of magically transforming anything he touched, however insignificant it might appear, as the street lamps in Plaza Real Square.

The Sacred Family Church, an unfinished symphony of stones and iron in a highly controversial but increasingly appreciated arrangement.

Gaudí's works are scattered all over the city, but their main core is situated in the modern part of Barcelona built in the 20th. century as a result of industrial expansion.

In chronological order, the first major work of Gaudí was Vicens house (1878-1880), situated at No. 24 of Carolinas Street. At the time, the architect was only 26 years old. Vicens house was followed in Barcelona by the beginning of the construction of the Sacred Family Church, a work on which he was busy until the end of his life and which was still left unfinished. On the other hand, it is unlikely that the enormous building will be finished in the near future, for according to the statues the work must only be financed by contributions from the public. One year after starting work on the Sacred Family Church, in 1885 he started work on Guell Palace which was completed in 1889. This palace today houses the Scenic Art

Detail of the central niche of the church.

Detail of one of the lateral niches of the church.

Museum. In 1887 he erected gates, pavillions and walls on the Guell estate, and two years later he started work on the school of Santa Teresa de Jesús. In 1898 he started at the same time the work on Calvet house and on the crypt of the church of the Guell development in Santa Coloma. In 1900, he also tackled simultaneously the work on Figueras house, more widely known as ''Bellesguard'', and on Guell park. The latter was completed in 1914, providing Barcelona with a truly revolutionary garden city. From the grille to the last stone — one of these stones which we do not know whether Gaudí planned it or whether it was left there by nature — we can feel the hand of a great artist far ahead of practically all the expressions of art of his time, some of which have not yet been followed up because many more years have to elapse before the work of Gaudí prompts us to action instead of leaving us inactive with astonishment. There is no doubt that Gaudí, as Le Corbusier put it, ''has been the most creative architect of his generation''

View of the Sacred Family Church, a masterpiece by Gaudí.

Entrance to Güell Park, a work showing Gaudí's skill in shaping the landscape.

The entrance to the Güell Park.

A partial view of the famous bench that, crookedly, runs over the esplanade of the Park.

Güell Park. Decorative soffit-work by J. Jujol —that is suspended below the square. A detail of the railing of the entrance and fragments of the bench.

A sculptural detail of a central element on the main staircase. ▷

In 1905, visibly used to doing two jobs at the same time, he started building Batlló house and Milá house, the latter being more widely known as "La Pedrera". And one year before completing "La Pedrera", possibly the most controversial of his works, he started building the schools of the Sacred Family. Gaudí died in 1926, victim of a traffic accident, an ironic end to the life of a man who had always followed the streets devised in his own mind.

The special world of Gaudí has one of its most characteristic expressions in the Casa Batlló.

General view of the façade of Milá house, more widely known as «La Pedrera». One of the most controversial works by the great Catalan architect.

TIBIDABO MOUNTAIN

The Tibidabo is part of the Collcerola range sheltering the city from cold northern winds. With its 500 metres altitude it commands a splendid view of Barcelona. Any visitor to the city should take the trouble to climb these 500 metres — naturally using his car or the funicular — because Tibi-

Aerial view of mount Tibidabo, spectacular viewpoint of the city and favourite recreational area thanks to the surrounding woods.

*Entrance to Sacred Heart Church
on the Tibidabo.*

dabo mountain is something more than a terrace over the city: The Tibidabo mountain not only offers its lofty Sacred Heart Church, the Fabra observatory and the museums of physical science and of tourism, it is above all an exciting fun fair with all the necessary amenities to spend a pleasant day of rest, which is welcomed by those who have been looking for days on end at ancient monuments and architecture.

FROM THE FEET OF COLUMBUS

Along the pages of this book, the reader has toured Barcelona using Columbus as a guide. Indeed, what better guide could there be! In fact, Barcelona begins and ends at Columbus' feet. It is like a great river with the Ramblas as its main river and with two major tributaries leading to the right and left, to Ciudadela park and Montjuich.

Turning his back to Columbus, thus escaping the peremptory gesture of his stretched arm —which seems to divert all the traffic of the city to the sea — the reader has started his tour along the main river, the Ramblas, and has then turned to the right to admire the monuments of the Gothic District as a keen student of art. Then, after completing his visit to the Gothic District, and after having reached Catalonia Square, he has gone back to the feet of Columbus to follow one of the tributaries which led him along Columbus Promenade to Ciudadela park after which, taking in many different aspects, he has reached the top of Tibidabo mountain after getting acquainted with the bullfight and the work of Gaudí.

Now a fresh discovery is waiting for him. He will now follow the second tributary which will lead him to Montjuich mountain.

Columbus memorial, with Reales Atarazanas on the right and Montjuïc castle in the background.

The caravel «Santa María», a reproduction of the one that was used to discover the New World. Curiously enough, Columbus and his ship, inseparable in their achievements, have come to land together in the port of Barcelona.

The Reales Atarazanas. Shipyard built under Peter IV in 1378.

Maritime Museum. Galleon of Don Juan de Austria.

THE REALES ATARAZANAS

The Reales Atarazanas is the only medieval shipyard which has survived in Europe. It was built under Peter IV in 1378 and was subsequently extended; the facade looking to the sea is from the 18th century.

Maritime Museum. Model of the «Ictineo» by Narciso Monturiol. Forerunner of the modern submarine.

Maritime Museum. The hall of the Marqués de Comillas.

THE PARALELO

On the Avenida del Marqués del Duero, more widely known under its former name of El Paralelo, the visitor may penetrate into some of the narrow adjacent streets to get an idea of what the so-called Chinese District — still known as such without reason — used to be. This is the typical centre of night life which is to be found in any city with a major port.

Likewise, the Paralelo is no longer the Montmartre of Barcelona as it was rightly known in former times, but as the Chinese District, it it still a place where a few very typical corners can be discovered.

The music-hall and theatres provide the animated night life of the famous Paralelo of Barcelona.

LICEO THEATRE

Going up the Ramblas on the left side, the visitor will find a building which, with unnecessary modesty, hides a sumptuous interior setting behind its ugly facade. The building is the Liceo Theatre, the world's best Opera house in terms of acoustics and the second most important — next to the Scala of Milan — in terms of capacity, as it accommodates 3,500 persons.

The construction of the Liceo Theatre which lasted four years started in 1844. Its first architect was Miguel Garriga y Roca, but he was not to remain the only one as the Liceo, possibly because it was regarded as a symbol of Catalan plutocracy, was to become the theatre of many bomb attacks. For some time it looked as if it had been chosen as a training ground by anarchists. There was hardly a follower of Proudhon who did not throw at least one bomb into the stalls. Finally, there was a big fire which destroyed most of the delicate Elizabethan decoration and the even more inflammable red tapestries.

Today the Liceo has recovered all the glamour of its best days. Once again, the gala shows at the Liceo draw Barcelona's high society which is as keen as it was yesterday on enjoying the art of the most renowned artists of opera and ballet.

The façade of the Gran Teatro del Liceo.

SAN PABLO DEL CAMPO

On the Paralelo, behind the Reales Atarazanas, after contemplating the remains of the Gothic fortification of the city, the visitor will find the church of the monastery of San Pablo del Campo, a construction from the early centuries of the Romanesque era.

On its modest site, somewhat overshadowed by the neighbouring buildings, the church of San Pablo del Campo raises its Romanesque silhouette noted for its compact and simple shape.

View of the cloister of the monastery of San Pablo del Campo.

MONTJUICH

Montjuich mountain, the city's seaside scenic viewpoint has its main entrance on Plaza de España. This entrance, flanked by two high towers, was built on the occasion of the International Exhibition of 1929 which was also the year of construction of the illuminated fountain designed by Buigas. This fountain, with its endless wealth of light and colour effects, gives a unique touch to summer nights in Barcelona. It was the first of the long series of fountains built by Buigas all over the world and which may one day reach its final climax in his theatre of water and light the design of which is already completed and which may be built one day in Barcelona as a last parade of increasingly difficult creations made by the great Catalan artist Buigas who combines water and light with music.

Leaving behind the enclosure of the trade fair and going up along the main avenue, the visitor will contemplate the splendid view of the National Palace.

The illuminated fountain of Buigas in today's trade fair enclosure.

To the lively beauty of the huge
illuminated fountain of Montjuïc,
Barcelona has added the static effect of
the projectors flashing into the
sky over the National Palace which
today houses the Museum of Catalan Art.

View of the Greek theatre.

The Congress Palace.

Mosén Jacinto Verdaguer Gardens.

CITY OF FAIRS
AND CONGRESSES

All over the world, Barcelona is known today as a city of fairs and congresses. This motto cannot be explained by the city's age-old commercial tradition alone. For Barcelona is not only the city which in 1888 organized the world fair, a city thus qualified for the most ambitious events. In addition to its skill in organization and to the existence of adequate facilities such as the trade fair enclosure of Montjuich and especially of its extremely modern Congress Palace and Palace of Fifty Years, the city provides additional features which contribute to the success of any fair or congress. These extra features are those which provide entertainment and a pleasant atmosphere as essential ingredients of any congress.

In Barcelona, participants of congresses and visitors of fairs not only find ideal conditions for their work, but also a city generously warmed by the Spanish sun, nearby beaches, unique museums, such as the museum of Romanesque art fascinating age-old monuments such as those of the Gothic District and the colourful night life of a Mediterranean city. Result: 50 international congress, 14 specialized trade fairs, the great trade fair in June and a total of two million visitors. This is the logical result of a city where visitors work, rest and enjoy themselves.

The Plaza de España is always busy at all hours.

Museum of Catalan Art. The Pantocrator. Fragment of the wall painting in the main apse of the Church of San Clemente de Tahull, Lérida. Regarded as the most valuable work of the 12th century.

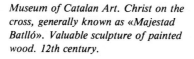

Museum of Catalan Art. Christ on the cross, generally known as «Majestad Batlló». Valuable sculpture of painted wood. 12th century.

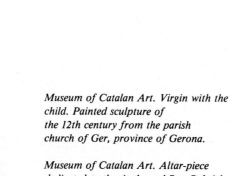

Museum of Catalan Art. Virgin with the child. Painted sculpture of the 12th century from the parish church of Ger, province of Gerona.

Museum of Catalan Art. Altar-piece dedicated to the Archangel San Gabriel. Detail of the Last Supper. From Soriguerola, in Urtx (Gerona). XIII-XIV Centuries.

MUSEUM OF CATALAN ART

Established in the National Palace of Montjuich, it is the world's most important museum in terms of Romanesque wall paintings and one of the best museums for Gothic altar paintings. The collection includes such remarkable works as the frontals of Los Obispos and Seo de Urgel, painted in the 12th century; the Majesty, a painted sculpture from the same century; the Pantocrator of San Clemente de Tahúll, regarded as the most valuable work from the 12th century; the reclining marble statue of Sibila de Fortiá, fourth wife of King Don Pedro the Ceremonious; the resurrection by Borrasá; the Virgin of the Milk by Ramón Mur; the admirable altar painting of Saint Vincent by the Catalan artist Bernat Martorell; the most popular altar painting ''Els Consellers'' by Luis Dalmau and many works by Jaime Huguet, the greatest Catalan painter of the second half of the 15th century.

The Museum of Catalan Art. A polychrome carving that represents the «Maiestas Domini» and on both sides, under arches, the twelve apostles. It is the frontal of an altar —XII century— that came from the parish church of Santa María de Tahull.

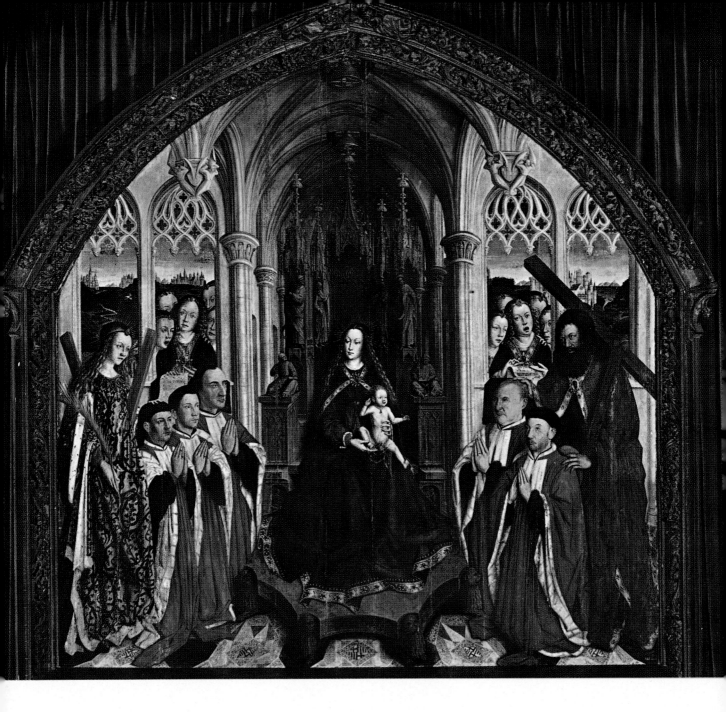

Museum of Catalan Art. The Virgin «dels Consellers», creation by Luis Dalmau (1445).

Apart from Romanesque and Gothic art mentioned so far, there are masterpieces of Spanish painting from the 16th to the 18th century, such as: Saint Peter and Saint Paul by El Greco; Saint Paul by Velázquez; portrait of a Dominican and Saint Francis of Assisi, both by Zurbarán; Saint Jerome by Ribalta and, apart from a work ascribed to Tintoretto, the Martyrdom of Saint Bartholomew, by Ribera.

*Spanish Village. Entrance
and general view.*

Spanish Village. The Prades fountain, Plaza de la Herradura (Córdoba) and craftsmen working in the presence of the public.

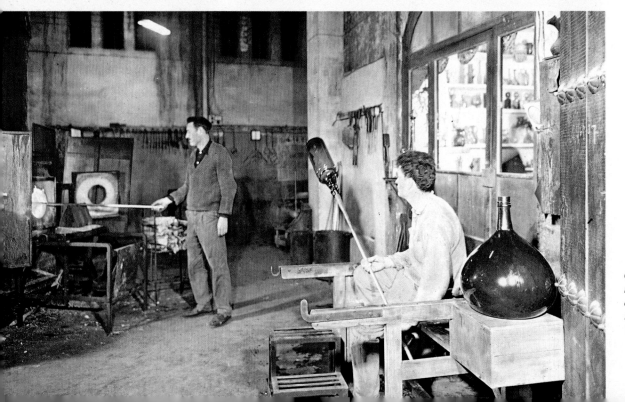

One of the most typical corners in the Spanish Village.

THE SPANISH VILLAGE

The Spanish Village, also built on the occasion of the world fair of 1929, is a work mainly due to the initiative of Miguel Utrillo and Xavier Nogués.

The Spanish Village, as its name suggests, is a full-size reproduction of the most typical styles and expressions of Spanish regional architecture. The entrance to the Village leads through the gate of Saint Vincent, a reproduction of the well-known city gate of Avila. This gate leads to Castile Square from which different streets lead to the individual provinces. This is to be taken literally, for a visit to the Spanish Village is a genuine visit to Spain. A magical visit because it provides a simultaneous overall view of the rich and often contradictory mosaic of Spanish architecture. A lively and tangible view for, to the different museums inside the village we have to add the many workshops where the tradesmen work in the presence of the public and sell their latest production as soon as it is completed.

Spanish Village. Typical Andalusian street.

The fun fair is a definite date not only for those looking for enjoyment, but also for those that want to enjoy one of the most beautiful panoramic views of the city.

Monument to the «sardana», a work by J. Cañas.

MONTJUICH CASTLE

Montjuich mountain is not only known for its splendid gardens designed by the Frenchman Forestier. The problem of Montjuich is that each of its places of interest is a point of attraction in its own right. Thus, a visit to Montjuich not only means to view what has already been described, but also to enjoy its sporting facilities, the splendid view from the natural watchtower of Miramar, to take a bird's eye view of the port from the aerial ropeway leading to Barceloneta; to visit the modern fun fair and the nearby dancing halls; to enjoy an open-air meal in hanging gardens between the sky and the sea; to admire the eternal art performed in the Greek open air theatre, and among many other delightful things, to visit the military museum established on top of the mountain in Montjuich castle, formerly a fortress and today a proud viewpoint commanding a panoramic view of the city.

Montjuïc. Like old dwellings on an enchanted mountain, you have here the impressive but inoffensive sight of venerable canons pointing the empty gaze of their eyes towards the city.

An exuberant and tropical nook of the new gardens of «Mossèn Costa i Llobera» decorating the road called Miramar that leads from the foot of the Port to the Mountain of Montjuïc.

Full view of Paseo de Gracia, spectacular main avenue of modern Barcelona.

MODERN BARCELONA

The increasing industrial and commercial development of Barcelona which reached its climax towards the end of the last century also resulted in a gradual expansion of the city which, on account of its geographical location, could take place only towards the slopes of

«Punxes» house by Puig i Cadafalch, a spectacular example of a vigorous and modern style.

An expansive view of the Diagonal.

mount Tibidabo. At that time Paseo de Gracia, thus named because it follows the old road which used to link Barcelona to the township of Gracia which today is part of Barcelona, started developing into the city's main avenue. Paseo de Gracia used to be the showroom of the works of the most celebrated architects, and even today, as modern Barcelona has ousted Paseo de Gracia to some extent, just as the latter had ousted the Ramblas at an earlier stage, the avenue still retains some very interesting features, although these are just a pale reflection of the splendid array of stately houses of former times.

Modern Barcelona is an extension of previously modernized districts, but with its direction clearly shifting to the west. Its main street, the former Diagonal, thus named because it cuts across the modern part of the city in diagonal direction, is Avenida del Generalísimo Franco, an avenue increasingly invaded by shops and office buildings. One of its side streets, Calle Tuset, is also popularly known as Barcelona's Carnaby Street.

A view of the Diagonal, at its intersection with Paseo de Gracia.

Barcelona Football Club's modern stadium.

A general view of the interior of the Barcelona Blaugrana Palace.

Calvo Sotelo Square. Junction between modern and supermodern Barcelona.

*Founded in 1326, the royal monastery
of Pedralbes is due to the initiative
of Queen Elisenda de Montcada,
fourth wife of Jaime II. This splendid
specimen of architecture is today inhabited
by Clarice nuns. The façade in the purest
medieval style conceals one of the most
pleasant and poetic interiors any walls can
enclose. The most impressing part in terms
of beauty and quiet is the cloister which
surrounds a patio with palm-trees
and a Renaissance well. No less remarkable
is the artistic beauty of the sepulchre
of the founder with its valuable recumbent
statue made of alabaster.*

Final stretch of the Diagonal where it becomes a freeway leading to the outskirts.

A panoramic view of the University area.

Modern Barcelona — the Barcelona which built the stadium of the local football club, one of the finest specimens of stadium architecture in the world — extends over the northwestern area of the city known as Sarriá and especially over the Pedralbes district where in symbolic coexistence the residential buildings with their functional design merge with the historical walls of the old royal monastery of Pedralbes. Thus, in a continous and consistent embrace, Barcelona tackles the future following the routes of the past.

*The biggest
contrasts and the
most different
aspects.
A miscellaneous
collection in
only one picture:
the city in fiestas.*

Contents

That ancient part of history which is Spain is often referred to as "the bull's skin", because that is the shape of Spain on the map. The aim of this book is to present a detailed and comprehensive picture of a fragment of that "bull's skin", and to help this it includes a number of spectacular photographs. The Editor will be well satisfied if he has succeeded in giving you a deeper and better knowledge of Spain.

The printing of this book was completed in the workshops of FISA - Industrias Gráficas, Palaudarias, 26 - Barcelona (Spain)